YOUR KNOWLEDGE HAS VALUE

Pranushka Naidoo

Should the UK leave the EU or consider an EEA relationship? A question of supremacy

GRIN Publishing

Bibliographic information published by the German National Library:

The German National Library lists this publication in the National Bibliography; detailed bibliographic data are available on the Internet at http://dnb.dnb.de .

Imprint:

Copyright © 2014 GRIN Verlag GmbH
Print and binding: Books on Demand GmbH, Norderstedt Germany
ISBN: 978-3-656-94867-4

This book at GRIN:

http://www.grin.com/en/e-book/298325/should-the-uk-leave-the-eu-or-consider-an-eea-relationship-a-question

GRIN - Your knowledge has value

Since its foundation in 1998, GRIN has specialized in publishing academic texts by students, college teachers and other academics as e-book and printed book. The website www.grin.com is an ideal platform for presenting term papers, final papers, scientific essays, dissertations and specialist books.

Visit us on the internet:

http://www.grin.com/

http://www.facebook.com/grincom

http://www.twitter.com/grin_com

SHOULD THE UK LEAVE THE EU OR CONSIDER AN EEA RELATIONSHIP? – A QUESTION OF SUPREMACY

By

Pranushka Naidoo

A DISSERTATION

Submitted to

The University of Liverpool

in partial fulfillment of the requirements
for the degree of

MASTER OF INTERNATIONAL BUSINESS LAW

28-04-2014

ACKNOWLEDGEMENTS

I thank my Lord God for giving me everything I needed to complete this dissertation, for with Him all things are possible. I would like to thank my beloved family: my loving parents, Annsey and Bernard, for educating me, encouraging me and supporting me throughout my life without you I would never have made it. To my beloved sister, Nisesha, thank you for being the best sister anyone could ever have. And to the most important person in my life, I thank my baby boy Matthew for being ever so patient with me while I completed my studies – I did this for you my Darling-Boy.

My appreciation and heartfelt thanks goes to my dissertation adviser Dr Sarah Fox, for her guidance, patience and time. I would also like to thank Dr Matilde Ventrella for her inspiration and the staff of University of Liverpool who have made my goal possible. Lastly, thank you MERW for your support.

God bless you all.

Pranushka Naidoo
New Zealand, April 2014

ABSTRACT

SHOULD THE UK LEAVE THE EU OR CONSIDER AN EEA RELATIONSHIP? – A QUESTION OF SUPREMACY!

By

Pranushka Naidoo

While the EU remains an attractive proposition for other European countries, such as the recent addition of Latvia as a Member State, the UK however does not regard Europe as a flourishing economy that it joined 40 years ago.

It is no secret that the euro-zone has suffered an economic crisis. This has lead to a lack of dynamism between Europe and the UK as countries that use the single currency are bound tighter together, leaving the British people insecure with regards to uncontrolled immigration issues and single EU market demands. Eurosceptics believe the UK should withdraw from the EU despite a lack of precedence for such an event. However, political leaders are of the opinion that the UK does not require to leave the EU but rather review the terms of EU relationship altogether.

This paper therefore contributes to the research of public international law by examining the issues surrounding the supremacy of the EU within the UK as a Member State, the withdrawal of the UK, with a view to its success and consequences/risks involved, the withdrawal process in terms of Article 50 of the Lisbon Treaty and the options available for the UK to continue its relationship with the EU or consider an EFTA or EEA relationship much to that of its counterparts such as Norway or to leave both the EU and the single market altogether, but attempt to recreate a free-trade relationship through bilateral agreements, similar to that of the Swiss model.

This research will therefore demonstrate the UK's position as an EU member and the challenges the UK faces with regards to its stability and future as a country within the global financial economy.

Keywords: EU supremacy, EEA relationship, EU member state, withdrawal

TABLE OF CONTENTS

Chapter 1.
INTRODUCTION

1.1   Scope

The European Union ('**EU**') is based on the rule of law[1] which means that any action taken by

the EU is initiated via the Treaties[2] that have been approved '*voluntarily and democratically*'[3]

by EU Member States. Thus by contrast should a particular policy area not be cited in any

Treaty, the European Commission cannot propose a law in that area[4].

A Treaty is defined as a binding agreement between EU Member States. It sets out EU

objectives and rules for EU institutions, and it contains the principles on how decisions are

made and the relationship between the EU and its Member States.

As time develops countries and policies develop. Subsequent to that, Treaties are amended

to make the EU more efficient and transparent, to prepare for new Member States and to

introduce areas of cooperation, for example in currency and trade[5]. Thus, for example, the

---

[1] Prof J.H.H., Weiler, '*The Rule of Law as a Constitutional Principle of the European Union*' Jean Monnet Working , Paper 04/09, < *www.jeanmonnetprogram.org/archive/papers/09/090401.doc*>
[2] The 'Treaties': *Treaty of Lisbon*, (signed: 13 December 2007, entered into force: 1 December 2009); *Treaty of Nice*, (signed: 26 February 2001, entered into force: 1 February 2003); *Treaty of Amsterdam* (signed: 2 October 1997, entered into force: 1 May 1999); *Treaty on European Union – Maastricht Treaty* (signed: 7 February 1992, entered into force: 1 November 1993); *Single European Act* (signed: 17 and 28 February 1986 (in Luxembourg and The Hague respectively), entered into force: 1 July 1987); *Merger Treaty – Brussels Treaty* (signed: 8 April 1965, entered into force: 1 July 1967); *Treaties of Rome – EEC and EURATOM treaties* (signed 25 March 1957 and entered into force: 1 January 1958); *Treaty establishing the European Coal and Steel Community* (signed: 18 April 1951, entered into force: 23 July 1952 – expired 23 July 2002).
[3] Prof J.H.H. Weiler, '*The Rule of Law as a Constitutional Principle of the European Union*' Jean Monnet, Working Paper 04/09, < *www.jeanmonnetprogram.org/archive/papers/09/090401.doc*>
[4] *Ibid*
[5] Prof J.H.H. Weiler, '*The Rule of Law as a Constitutional Principle of the European Union*' Jean Monnet Working Paper 04/09, < *www.jeanmonnetprogram.org/archive/papers/09/090401.doc*>

'FT'[6] would have to be amended to include Member States and any subsequent changes when a new Member State joins the EU[7].

Under the Treaties[8], EU institutions can adopt legislation, which the Member States then implement within their own legal systems.

Europe can no longer be described thriving economic club that Britain joined 40 years ago. It is no secret that the euro-zone has suffered an economic crisis giving way to a lack of dynamism between Europe and Britain. As countries are brought closer together sharing a single currency it leaves the British feeling insecure about the uncontrolled immigration issues and single EU market demands. According to recent political news[9], political leaders are determined to stop a UK exit however there are mixed views as to the UK's position[10].

While the possibility of a UK exit exists, UK politicians are of the opinion that this relationship is a commitment – a likeness to that of marriage – and it should be left alone to develop with all partners contributing to the process given that a UK withdrawal could be viewed as being counter-productive.

The EU relationship is based on Treaties, and the terms and conditions of the relationship, like any union, allow for a Member State's commitment to be broken[11]. The terms and conditions of an EU relationship set out objectives, rules and guidelines as to legislative decisions that are relative to the relationships forged between the EU and those subsequent relations between Member States.

---

[6] The Founding Treaties ('FT') being *Treaty establishing the European Coal and Steel Community* (1951); *Treaty establishing European Economic Community* (1957); *Treaty establishing the European Atomic Energy Community* (1957); *Treaty on European Union* (1992).

[7] EU Union, '*EU Treaties*' <*http://europa.eu/about-eu/basic-information/decision-making/treaties/index_en.htm*> (accessed on: 17/2/2014)

[8] *Ibid* and footnote 2 above

[9] A. Kaletsky, 'Will Britain leave the European Union' Reuters, (16 Jan 2014) <http://blogs.reuters.com/anatole-kaletsky/2014/01/16/will-britain-really-leave-the-european-union/>

[10] Britain and Europe: Making the break, The Economist (8 Dec 2012) <http://www.economist.com/news/briefing/21567914-how-britain-could-fall-out-european-union-and-what-it-would-mean-making-break>

[11] As provided for in terms of Article 50 of the Lisbon Treaty

This inadvertently means that Member States allow for a 'cooperative[12]' aspect on matters such as home affairs, justice (pillar 3) and territory[13] between themselves, thereby promoting EU rights of cross-border trade[14] and freedom of movement[15]. However there is always the risk that should one of the Member States feel threatened by an influx of trade from foreigners, there could be a need to withdraw from said Treaties.

Cooperation, by example, between Member States for consumer protection, deals with the issue of cross-border purchases whereby consumers are protected against the odd chance of rogue traders. This cooperation between Member States was put in place to ensure the application of legislation on consumer protection within the internal market was effective enough to avoid future problems[16]. An example of this *cooperation* was found in the preamble to the Rome Treaty wherein it was mentioned it would have an 'ever closer' union amongst the undersigned parties[17]. UK politicians, however, took an adverse stand to the

---

12 Summaries of European Legislation, 'Treaty of Maastricht on European Union' (2010): The Maastricht Treaty has a complicated structure wherein its preamble is sets out seven titles as follows: "Title I contains provisions shared by the Communities, common foreign policy, and judicial cooperation. Title II contains provisions amending the EEC Treaty, while Titles III and IV amend the ECSC and EAEC Treaties respectively. Title V introduces provisions concerning common foreign and security policy (CFSP). Title VI contains provisions on cooperation in the fields of justice and home affairs (JHA). The final provisions are set out in Title VII of the Treaty". <http://europa.eu/legislation_summaries/institutional_affairs/treaties/treaties_maastricht_en.htm>

[13] J.M. Magone, 'The end of the borders? The politics of territorial cooperation in the multi-level governance system. A comparative study of cross-border cooperation initiative' Berlin School of Economics & Law (2010)
< http://www.aecpa.es/uploads/files/congresos/congreso_09/grupos-trabajo/area02/GT01/08.pdf>

[14] Article 34 TFEU; Free movement of goods: Guide to the application of Treaty provision governing the free movement of goods', European Commissions Director of Enterprise and Industry (2010), pg10 < http://ec.europa.eu/enterprise/policies/single-market-goods/files/goods/docs/art34-36/new_guide_en.pdf>

[15] Article 45 TFEU; *'Free movement of goods: Guide to the application of Treaty provision governing the free movement of goods'*, European Commissions Director of Enterprise and Industry (2010), pg 31 < http://ec.europa.eu/enterprise/policies/single-market-goods/files/goods/docs/art34-36/new_guide_en.pdf>

[16] *Regulation (EC) No 2006/2004 of the European Parliament and of the Council of 27 October 2004 on cooperation between national authorities responsible for the enforcement of consumer protection laws (the Regulation on consumer protection cooperation) [See amending act(s)].*
<http://europa.eu/legislation_summaries/consumers/protection_of_consumers/l32047_en.htm>

[17] Rome Treaty 1957, Title 1, 'Common Provisions, Article 1
< http://eur-lex.europa.eu/en/treaties/dat/12002M/htm/C_2002325EN.000501.html>

3

statement and confirmed that the treaty only ensured certain key areas of practical cooperation, such as trade[18].

While joining the EU was for the economic benefit, there were also political benefits. Perhaps it would be better suited for the UK to be outside the EU while still participating politically similar to that of Norway, or Switzerland, whether in the UN, NATO, the WTO, the IMF or simply in specific multilateral and bilateral relationships[19]. It would be most beneficial for its economy however if the UK instead stayed within the EU but altered its terms and conditions of membership. This would guarantee its protection for the freedom of movement of goods under Article 35 of the TFEU. For example, in the case of *Cassis de Dijon*[20] the CJEU established the principle of mutual recognition whereby goods from domestic and foreign traders that are produced and manufactured lawfully by a Member State should circulate freely within the Union without hindrance. The CJEU found that imported goods should not be modified to a host country's requirements and deemed such measures as being unlawful because they are likely to incur unnecessary expenses.

1.2   Outcome

However if the UK does not decide to stay, much has to be considered for the UK to withdraw. Factors such as the economy, trade, ease of movement, and the legal aspects of the legal system being affected by EU-supremacy will be discussed in order to ascertain the conclusion of the UK's status from here on end.

---

[18] P. Minford, V. Mahambare, and E. Nowell, '*Should Britain Leave the EU? An Economic Analysis of a Troubled Relationship*' <http://www.euro-know.org/eu_book/index.php>
[19] *Ibid*, pg 3
[20] *Rewe Zentrale v Bundesmonopolverwaltung für Branntwein* ('**Cassis de Dijon**') [1979] ECR 649

While the *Factortame I* case held that EU law is supreme within the UK[21], the question to be answered, however, is to what extent is its supremacy powerful enough to dissuade the UK from leaving and would this be to its advantage from an economic and political perspective. Thus the scope of this thesis will formulate an opinion of the EU's supreme part within the UK and the effect it has had on the country and its legal system. The question of the EU's supremacy and integrity of its relationship with the UK as it plans to 'separate' itself from a once happy EU marriage will also be considered. A conclusion will be reached as to whether it is viable for the UK to be a part of the EU and the pros and cons to its existence within the EU as compared to that of its counterparts[22].

A research report by the House of Commons, Foreign Affairs Committee[23] has suggested that the UK would be better placed having an European Economic Area (EEA)-like relationship and should take note of the following points:

1. The UK should leave the EU's protective agreements altogether *inter alia*, tariffs and anti-dumping and resume a unilateral free trade agreement. While this would put the UK outside the EU's protective arrangements, it would have the same access to the EU market as any WTO non-EU member. EU members would have the same free access to the UK market as any EEA member.

2. Where services are concerned, (the UK which already has a large free trade and free market entry), the Single Market could bring about competition and the UK can

---

[21] C-213/89 *Factortame I* [1990] ECR I-2433, A duty is placed on national courts to secure the full effectiveness of Community law, even where it is necessary to create a national remedy where none previously existed. The House of Lords accepted supremacy of EU law in this case. This is important in context of British Parliamentary Sovereignty. Lord Bridge held that Parliament had voluntarily accepted this limitation of its sovereignty, being fully aware that, even if the limitation of sovereignty was not inherent in the EEC Treaty, it had been well established by jurisprudence before Parliament passed the European Communities Act of 1972

[22] V. Miller, 'Leaving the EU' Research Paper 13/42, House of Commons Library (1 July 2013) <*www.parliament.uk/briefing-papers/RP13-42.pdf*>

[23] V. Miller, 'Leaving the EU' Research Paper 13/42, House of Commons Library (1 July 2013) <www.parliament.uk/briefing-papers/RP13-42.pdf>

participate in such discussions and cooperate on a case-by-case basis to create new agreements.

3.	The UK should continue with the arrangement of having the freedom of movement of capital, labour, goods and services given that this arrangement has brought about benefits.

4.	The UK should continue to participate in all areas concerning competition policy, economic consultations, and coordination of anti-terrorist policies.

5.	Lastly, the supremacy of EU law would no longer be enforceable upon the UK neither will it be binding.	In that event, it would be more convenient that only those agreements that are explicitly made with the EU as any treaty obligation, be respected and incorporated into UK law.

Chapter 2.
THE ROLE OF EU, ITS PURPOSE AND EFFECTS ON THE UK'S LEGAL SYSTEM

2.1   The EU - European Community - European Communities

The EU has been described as a distinct economic and political organization of 28 democratic European countries. It became the EU in 1993 and when the Treaty of Lisbon entered into force on 1 December 2009, the EU then replaced the European Community which had existed since 1958, and took over all remaining duties, rights and obligations[24].

The EU's roots stem from the European Communities. The European Communities, which is originally referred to as the European Economic Community ('**EEC**') and the European Atomic Energy Community ('**Euratom**'), were both formed in 1958, while the European Coal and Steel Community ('**ECSC**'), was formed in 1952[25].

The European Union was created by the Treaty of Maastricht in 1992 and the Treaty of Amsterdam 1997[26] (both are commonly referred to as the Treaty on European Union (TEU)). It consisted of three pillars: the community dimension (EEC/EC, ECSC, Euratom), the common foreign and security policy, and a common cooperation in the field of justice and home affairs. The European Economic Community was renamed the European Community. It covered certain policy areas of the EU, such as Union citizenship, Community policies and Economic and Monetary Union (EMU).

---

[24] M. Newman, '*Concepts and Confusions*', Democracy, Sovereignty and the European Union, London: Hurst & Company, 1996, p.3
[25] *Ibid*
[26] S. Hanson, 'Chapter 5: Reaching English Law – The European Dimension', Legal Method and Reasoning, 2nd Ed., 2003, p.131

In 2009, by way of the Treaty of Lisbon, the three-pillar structure was abolished and the European Community was absorbed by the EU[27].

While the Euratom continues to exist as a legally distinct entity from the EU, the Euratom and the EU, however, have an equal number of member states and share the same institutions. It acts in several areas connected with atomic energy, including research, the drawing up of safety standards, and the peaceful uses of nuclear energy. The European Coal and Steel Community ceased to exist in 2002, when the ECSC Treaty expired[28].

It should be noted however that when it comes to the power of making law, the EU has no law making powers outside those conferred by the founding treaties of the European Community, however for the purpose of this research paper the phrase 'EU law' will be used interchangeably with Community law or European Community law ('**EC law**').

2.2   The accession of the UK to the EU

The UK joined the EU via, the Treaty of Accession 1972 ('TA'), an agreement between the European Communities and four countries (Denmark, Ireland, Norway and the United Kingdom)[29].   The TA entered into force on 1 January 1973 thereby allowing the aforementioned countries to obtain accession to the European Community and this became an important part of the constitutional grounds of the EU[30].   On reflection, it was from this point that the EU (or as it was known then, the European Communities) had taken on the position of becoming a supreme authority in the eyes of the UK.

---

[27] M. Newman 'Concepts and Confusions, Democracy, Sovereignty and the European Union', 1996, London: Hurst & Company, p.3

[28] *Ibid*

[29] Official Journal Council Regulation (EC) *OJ L 73 of 7.3.1972, p. 3* < http://eur-lex.europa.eu/LexUriServ/LexUriServ.do?uri=OJ:L:1972:073:FULL:EN:PDF>

[30] Official Journal of the European Communities Legislation, Special Edition, 27 March 1972 <http://eur-lex.europa.eu/LexUriServ/LexUriServ.do?uri=OJ:L:1972:073:FULL:EN:PDF>

2.3 Historical development of the European Community & European Community law

At first, the UK was seen to have no interest in joining the European Community in 1957. Instead, it went ahead with setting up the European Free Trade Area ('**EFTA**') with Austria, Denmark, Norway, Portugal, Sweden and Switzerland[31]. While this manoeuvre could have been viewed as a defensive move by European States, not in the EEC at the time, all of the original members of EFTA with the exception of Norway (due to a public referendum held to not join the European Community) became members of the European Community (now the EU). However, after four years, the UK decided to change its policy and proceeded to apply for membership but France blocked the application for just over 10 years. Then, in 1972 the UK signed and ratified the Treaty of Accession[32].

The nature of the European Community is founded on the Treaty of Rome which insists on its provisions being enforced by the legal systems of Member States. The UK had to adopt parts of the Treaty into English law through the enactment of the European Communities Act 1972[33].

The idea for the Member States coming together under one 'umbrella' was primarily based on the usefulness of obtaining an economic unity[34], that is the EU, to forge a greater political and social community[35]. The desire for a broader EU area was initially based on a need for materials, movement of people, goods and trade. This need was placed on agenda and advanced by the Single European Act 1986 which secured the economic future for a single currency — the euro.

---

[31] A. Aust, '*Chapter 23: The European Union*' Handbook of International Law, 2nd Ed. 2010, Cambridge University Press, p.430

[32] M. Newman '*Concepts and Confusions*', Democracy, Sovereignty and the European Union, 1996, London: Hurst & Company, p.3

[33] S. Hanson, '*Chapter 5*: Reaching English Law – The European Dimension', Legal Method and Reasoning, 2nd Ed., 2003, p.132

34 K. A. Mingst, , I. M., Arreguín-Toft '*Chapter 7: Intergovernmental Organizations, Nongovernmental Organizations, and International Law | Essentials of International Relations*', 5 Ed., September 2010 < http://www.wwnorton.com/college/polisci/essentials-of-international-relations5/ch/07/summary.aspx>

[35] *Ibid*, p.132

The EU was created in 1992 by the Member States of the European Community concluding the TEU 1992, (also known as the Maastricht Treaty). This Treaty, *vis-à-vis* the Union, has an international level of operation; however, it does not affect any of the legal systems of Member States. But should the EU operate, through its institutions, within the legislative capacity of the European Community, those actions do have an effect on the legal systems of Member States[36].

To explain further, if an area within the broader spectrum of the EU were to require defined perimeters to be embedded into the Member States' legal systems of the European Community, then and in that event, an agreement facilitating a move of matters from the EU into the sphere of legal competency of the European Community would have to occur. For example, an agreement had to be made between Member States of the EU to *co-operate* on matters of home affairs and justice (pillar 3) to be moved into the legal competency of the European Community so that it could become the subject of law making processes that was effective within the legal systems of Member States[37].

2.4   The nature of the EU

The main principle of the Treaty of Rome 1957 was to maintain a common economic and social progress towards a unified system. From this principle follows a series of other principles which are aimed at uniting the Member States for a greater more established purpose of social, economic and legal union. The Treaty specifically provides that it is aiming to lay 'the foundations of an ever closer union'[38].

---

[36] *Ibid, p.132*
[37] B.Vaughan, , '*An Analysis of EU Governance and Policy Making*', National Economic & Social Development Office NESDO, p.12 and p.27
[38] Europa, '*The Treaty on the Functioning of the European Union*', Official Journal of the EU, (Consolidated version), 9 May 2008, C115/49 < http://eur-

It should be remembered that the EU is not a designated geographical place, but rather an area for the purposes of Member States trading and relating financially, legally, politically, socially and culturally with one another. It could be said that the Community is a designated invisible market place, for a people who are united in their differences[39].

With the introduction of the EU came the idea of an established more specific supra-national legal and political order that each Member State agreed to be part of and bound by. In so agreeing, some aspects of sovereign rule within a Member State would need to be subject to the decisions of the supreme European legal and political institutions[40]. While the UK has anxiety as to its principle of sovereignty being subordinate to the EU (as will be explained below), each Member State in the EU remains separate, and this is an accepted state of fact within the wider group of the European Union[41].

2.5   Supremacy of the EU

As explained above, the Member State is a separate entity but unified under the umbrella of the EU. Thus while the principle of supremacy of Community law over national law in the Member States is an unwritten one, no Treaty has expressed that Community law should take precedence over national law neither is it a principle that was endorsed by any subsequent Treaty amendments. The Treaties are therefore said to be silent on the issue of the relationship between conflicting national law and Community law. However, it is an important part of the legal order of the EU[42].

---

lex.europa.eu/LexUriServ/LexUriServ.do?uri=OJ:C:2008:115:0047:0199:EN:PDF> (accessed 1 March 2014)
[39] B. Vaughan, 'An Analysis of EU Governance and Policy Making', National Economic & Social Development Office NESDO, p.28
[40] K. Archick 'The European Union: Questions and Answers' Congressional Research Service, January 15, 2014, p.1
[41] D. Edward 'EU Law and the Separation of Member States', 36 Fordham Int'l L.J. 1151 (2013)
[42] M. Stiernstrom, 'The Relationship between Community Law and National Law' The Jean Monnet Chair University of Miami, Miami Florida (October 2005)

The CJEU persists with its decision of complete supremacy of EU law over national law[43]. Craig & De Burca[44] explain that *"the aim of creating a uniform common market between different states would be undermined if Community law could be made subordinate to the national law of various states[45]"*. While the principle of supremacy is an unwritten rule of Community law and does not apply to the second and third pillars of the EU[46], it has evolved through the jurisprudence of the ECJ via case law.

In *Internationale Handelsgesellschaft mbH v. Einfuhr – und Vorratsstelle fur Getreide und Futtermittelthe[47] ('**Internationale Handelsgesellschaft**')*, the ECJ held that EU law must take precedence over any conflicting domestic law of Member States and decided that the validity of a Community measure or its effect within a Member State cannot be affected by any allegation that it opposed fundamental rights or principles that were formed via the constitutional law of that Member State[48].

This however has created clashes between Community law and national law, as will be explained below.

To explain the phenomenon of supremacy of EU laws over a Member State's national laws, the following questions are considered: 1) When a Member State becomes a said member of the EU and international conventions (which create new EU laws), is it possible to ratify such a convention when it contains those rules which would then contravene the Member State's Constitution; and 2) When the Member State has ratified such international convention and its EU laws, can the Member State's Constitution have supremacy over these EU laws.

---

[43] (Case 6/64) Costa v ENEL [1964] ECR 585
[44] P. Craig and P. De Burca, "EU Law Test, Cases and Materials", (4th Edition) Oxford University Press, 2007, p.344.
[45] (Case 106/77), Amministrazione delle Finanze dello Stato v. Simmenthal SpA [1978] ECR 629
[46] K-D.Borchardt, 'The ABC of Community Law', Official Publication of the European Communities, 2000, p. 24
[47] (Case 228/69), Internationale Handelsgesellschaft mbH v. Einfuhr und Vorratsstelle für Getreide und Futtermittel [1970] ECR 1125; [1972] CMLR 255
[48] *Ibid*

In an *Opinion on the 4th Amendment of the Constitution of Hungary*[49] it was provided that while *'domestic case laws have, on their part, considered that in certain cases the constitutional requirements could prevail over the law of the European Union'* while the German Constitutional Court in its decision[50] considered that *"the authorization to transfer some sovereign rights to the international institutions "is not of an unlimited nature at a constitutional level".* This provision therefore does not allow for the abandonment *"of the specific nature of the constitutional order which is in force in the Federal Republic of Germany, to interfere with its foundations, or its fundamental structures, by transferring sovereign rights to international institutions"*[51].

However, if the Court accepted that it should not review the fundamental rights which are respected by EU law *"it was only as long as the European Communities and the EU's precedents, constitute an efficient protection of the fundamental rights against the authorizes of the Communities, a protection considered as essentially comparable to the protection required by the fundamental law",* as a consequence if this was not the case, then it would exercise its right to a control. This position was confirmed in the Court's decision of 12 October 1993, in relation to the Maastricht Treaty where it stated that: *"the Constitutional Court will verify whether the acts of the European institutions and bodies were adopted within the scope of the sovereignty rights conferred upon them, or whether they fall outside of this scope"*[52].

To avoid any instance of conflict, these principles founded by the CJEU have created a 'set of rules' to indicate which legal norm shall prevail over the other. This has left the reception of the doctrine of supremacy in the Member States as slightly unwelcome[53]. Nevertheless case law has allowed for a development of the principle of supremacy of the EU over a Member

---

[49] F. Delperee *et al*, 'Opinion on the 4th Amendment of the Constitution of Hungary' (2011), p.9 < http://www.kormany.hu/download/d/e0/e0000/Traduc%20-%20opinion%20on%204th%20amendment.pdf>
[50] Extract from the German Constitutional Court's Maastricht Judgment of 12 October 1993, BVerfGE [89] p155 at pp 186 and 188
[51] *Ibid*
[52] *Ibid*
[53] E. Boomberg, and A. Stubb,. *'The European Union: How Does It Work'*, Oxford; New York: Oxford University Press, 2003, p. 62

State in cases such as: *Costa v ENEL*[54], *Internationale Handelsgesellschaft*[55] and *Simmenthal*[56].

Thus the extent to which the law of the EU and European Conventions has primacy over the Member States and their Constitutions can be evidenced by the answers the CJEU has given in the following cases:

In *Costa v ENEL*[57], *'The law stemming from the treaty, an independent source of law, could not, because of its special and original nature, be overridden by domestic legal provisions, however framed, without being deprived of its character as community law and without the legal basis of the community itself being called into question; ... the transfer by the states from their domestic legal system to the community legal system of the rights and obligations arising under the Treaty carries with it a permanent limitation of their sovereign rights, against with a subsequent unilateral act incompatible with the concept of the community cannot prevail';*

Then in, *Internationale Handelsgesellschaft*[58] the CJEU held that:

'3. Recourse to the legal rules or concepts of national law in order to judge the validity of measures adopted by the institutions of the Community would have an adverse effect on the uniformity and efficacy of Community law. The validity of such measures can only be judged in the light of Community law. In fact, the law stemming from the Treaty, an independent source of law, cannot because of its very nature be overridden by rules of national law, however framed, without being deprived of its character as Community law and without the legal basis of the Community itself being called in question. Therefore the validity of a Community measure or its effect within a Member State cannot be affected by allegations

---

[54] (Case 6/64) Flaminio Costa v ENEL [1964] ECR 585, CMLR 425,593
[55] (Case 228/69), Internationale Handelsgesellschaft mbH v. Einfuhr und Vorratsstelle für Getreide und Futtermittel [1970] ECR 1125; [1972] CMLR 255
[56] (Case106/77), Simmenthal II [1978] ECR 629
[57] (Case 6/64) Flaminio Costa v ENEL [1964] ECR 585, CMLR 425,593
[58] (Case 228/69), Internationale Handelsgesellschaft mbH v. Einfuhr und Vorratsstelle für Getreide und Futtermittel [1970] ECR 1125; [1972] CMLR 255

that it runs counter to either fundamental rights as formulated by the constitution of that State or the principles of a national constitutional structure'.

Furthermore in the *Simmenthal*[59] case, the CJEU confirmed that in general terms *'any provision of a national legal system … which might impair the effectiveness of community law … are incompatible with those requirements which are the very essence of community law'* – this decision covers the aspect of a supremacy of the EU laws over a Member State's constitutional provisions

EU case law therefore provides that the laws of the Community take precedence over any conflicting laws within the Member States. This means all national courts are obliged to ensure the practical effectiveness of supremacy by upholding Community law.

2.6   Supremacy of the EU over the UK

To give effect to EU law it was necessary for the UK to ratify EU law within its domestic legal system, by Parliament adopting EU law and promulgating the European Communities Act 1972 ('EC Act 1972'). Section 2(1) of the EC Act 1972 provides that all directly effective EU law will be automatically enforceable upon UK Courts[60] to the extent that *"All such rights, powers, liabilities, obligations and restrictions…and all such remedies and procedures…as in accordance with the Treaties are without further enactment to be given legal effect or used in the United Kingdom shall be recognized and available in law and be enforced, allowed and followed accordingly…'*[61]

---

[59] (Case106/77), Simmenthal II [1978] ECR 629
[60] I. Loveland, "Parliamentary Sovereignty and the European Community: The Unfinished Revolution?" Parliamentary Affairs, Oct. 1996, Vol. 49, Issue 4, p.517
[61] EU Communities Act 1972, c.68, Part 1, Section 2
<http://www.legislation.gov.uk/ukpga/1972/68/section/2 (accessed 23 January 2014);
EUR-Lex, *'Accession to the European Communities of the Kingdom of Denmark, Ireland, the Kingdom of Norway and the United Kingdom of Great Britain and Northern Ireland'* OJ L 73 27.3.1972 <http://eur-lex.europa.eu/JOHtml.do?uri=OJ:L:1972:073:SOM:EN:HTML>

However there is an underlying problem in the UK's acceptance of EU law as supreme law and that is the constitutional doctrine of parliamentary sovereignty. This doctrine states that *"Parliament is the supreme legal authority in the UK which can create or end any law"*[62] It is a legal norm that UK courts cannot overrule legislation of Parliament, and no Parliament can pass laws that future Parliament may not change. While the EC Act 1972 has imposed an obligation on the UK courts to act in accordance with EU law, Parliament can still repeal said Act.

In the series of the *Factortame*[63] cases the ECJ ruled that under the terms of the EC 1972 Act it was the duty of the UK courts, when delivering judgment in a case, to override any rule of national law found to be in conflict with directly enforceable and applicable EU law. The significance of the *Factortame*[64] cases are that the supremacy of EU law over national law of the UK is only recognized where EU law has competence over the UK legal system.

Thus if Parliament passes law which is in contradiction of EU law the national courts may grant a temporary order to prevent the UK authorities from enforcing said law. With that said, it should be noted that the supremacy of EU law is not derived from the special nature developed by the CJEU but by the employment of the parliamentary sovereignty doctrine which Parliament used to create the EC Act 1972[65].

Another example of the problem(s) the UK has with EU supremacy is indicated in recent matters with Member States concerning the implementation of EU Data Protection Regulations[66] where small and medium businesses were concerned. The UK objected to the EU's proposal to implement a 'one size fits all approach' where the compliance costs to

---

[62] Lord Irvine, *"Sovereignty in Comparative Perspective: Constitutionalism in Britain and America"*, New York University Law Review, Vol.76, Issue 1, April 2001, p.1
[63] *Factortame Ltd. v Secretary of State for Transport* [1991] 1 AC 603, 658
[64] *Ibid*
[65] M Dougan *"Who Exactly Benefits from the Treaties? The Murky Interaction Between Union and National Competence Over the Capacity to Enforce EU Law"* Cambridge Yearbook of European Legal Studies, Vol 12 (2009-2010) pp 73-120
66 Article 288 of the TFEU explains that EU Regulations shall have general application. It shall be binding in its entirety and directly applicable in all Member States

employ such a system are concerned[67]. The UK's main concern was that while the Impact Assessment report reflected that a single data protection statute across the Member States would save EUR2.3 billion a year, the EU regulation will have a negative impact on the UK's digital economy[68]

From case law it is apparent that there are tensions present when there is a direct conflict between EU law and UK law. For instance, in the case of *Macarthys Ltd v Wendy Smith*[69],.Smith had worked for Macarthys and claimed she was paid unequally compared her predecessor who was in the position before her. Marcarthys Ltd argued she had no claim because the UK's Equal Pay Act 1970 did not allow for salary comparisons with former colleagues. However, Smith argued that, if this was so under UK law, then EC law would operate since it allowed for such a comparison, and it would override the UK statute. The Court then considered the inconsistency between the Equal Pay Act 1970 and Article 119 of the EEC Treaty, concerning the Equal Treatment Directive. Lord Denning found (minority judgment) that *'whenever there is any inconsistency, Community law has priority'; after referring the case to the CJEU, it was held that the statute was inconsistent with the Treaty – the UK Act did not sufficiently promote the EU philosophy of equal pay for equal work. The CJEU considered a teleological approach to the Treaty and it was therefore necessary to look beyond the literal meaning of the statute to avoid incompatibility'*. The Court resolved the conflict by extending the interpretation of UK law to fit the European approach. As applied by Lord Denning, Article 119 of the Treaty clearly stated that Community law prevailed over UK law as it was the Court's *'bounden duty to give priority to Community law'*[70].

The apparent difficult relationship the UK has been experiencing between its sovereignty principle and the doctrine of EU supremacy is clear. The ability of the UK Parliament being

---

[67] L.R. Christensen *et al* 'The Impact of the Data Protection Regulation in the E.U.' *The European Financial Review*, (18 Jun 2013) < http://www.europeanfinancialreview.com/?p=6885>
[68] *Ibid*
[69] *Macarthys Ltd v Wendy Smith* [1980] EUECJ R-129/79 (27 March 1980)
[70] *Ibid*

empowered to perceive the operation of EU supremacy, gives room for the UK to either limit the EU's dominance or exit the EU altogether.

Chapter 3.
THE EU ASSISTED THE UK FOR THE BETTER

3.1 EU supremacy assisted the UK for a greater and stronger EU internal market

When the EU was founded in 1958 as the European Economic Community, one of its goals entailed creating a customs union and common market place for agriculture. Subsequently, this market was extended to cover goods and services within a common single market, which was largely completed by 1993[71]; this process also included a common currency, the euro.

There have been many 'pros' to the rule of the EU. The issue of supremacy of the EU over its Member States was not relevant for the purposes of the economic benefits of a unified collaboration and European integration. This clearly outweighed the expenses that would be borne for the creation of EU regulation[72]. Europe is said to have a single market of over 500 million people with an expansive free trade and capital movement area inclusive of open borders[73].

The EU protects its Member States by affording them the protection of its trade areas against any forms of rent-seeking, such as tariffs and quotas. On the other hand is attaches a large expense component to discourage any national interest groups who would lobby for EU-wide trade restrictions against outside countries[74]. This provides for a balanced global trade and an even playing field. However, the process is dependent on those that are in power within the EU institutions at the time these perimeters are put in place.

---

[71] Economic and Financial Affairs, ' The euro: Economic and Monetary Union January European Commission, (17 January 2014) <http://ec.europa.eu/economy_finance/euro/emu/index_en.htm>
[72] *Ibid*
[73] A Matthews, "How Might the EU's Common Agricultural Policy Affect Trade and Development After 2013?". (December 2010). ICTSD. < http://ictsd.org/i/publications/97803/>
[74] D. Vasishev, 'Contrary to Perception, the EU is a Boon to Free Markets' *Forbes* March 2013, <http://www.forbes.com/sites/realspin/2014/03/17/contrary-to-perception-the-european-union-is-a-boon-to-free-markets/>

The expense of regulation and the risks of centralization are not of great weight where such transparent economic openness exists.

When it came to the UK integrating EU law into the UK, the top most 100 European regulations cost the UK, approximately £27 billion[75]. Therefore, in order for the UK to separate itself from the EU it would have to transfer most of these regulations back to national level, but without abolishing it. The net cost of this venture would be within 1% of the GDP[76].

Given the rise of newly sustained economic and political powers, the EU provides a basis and forum for the UK to develop a common approach for key issues of mutual concern with the emerging economies and markets of Brazil, Russia, India and China. EU membership has allowed Member States to gain an increased political influence in relation to these areas and it does not restrict their ability to promote their exports to the aforementioned countries[77].

In all economic and political discussions, the UK is a part of the decision-making process as a Member State of the EU. It is interesting to note that the EU has supremacy on the rules of conduct for the UK's exit in terms of how the UK conducts itself when negotiating the terms and conditions within the EU's withdrawal agreement with the UK[78]. Thus when making its decision to leave the EU, the UK should take note of some of the difficulties other countries have experienced when they decided to stay out of the EU, but continue to have a trading relationship with it[79]. Examples of such countries are Norway and Switzerland, who are

---

[75] *Ibid*

[76] *Ibid*

[77] 'European Movement UK: The Wider Benefits of UK Membership of the EU' (February 2012) Euromove,

[78] As provided for by the Vienna Convention on the law of Treaties, Section 3 Termination and suspension of the Operation of Treaties, Article 54, 'Termination of or withdrawal from a treaty under its provision or by consent of the parties', (23 May 1969)

[79] D. Buchan, 'Outsiders on the inside – Swiss and Norwegian lessons for the UK' Centre for European Reform (September 2012)
<http://www.cer.org.uk/sites/default/files/publications/attachments/pdf/2012/buchan_swiss_norway_1 1oct12-6427.pdf>

nearly always bound by many EU decisions but are not party to them[80]. However although, Switzerland is not in the EEA, it has still agreed to voluntarily adopt many EU rules on the single market without having a say in its decision-making[81].

An official inquiry into Norway's EEA membership found that one of the problems Norway had with this form of membership with the EU is that Norway has to abide by and is bound to adopt EU policies and rules on a broad range of issues without being a part of the decision-making process and without the right to vote. This raises some democratic problems as Norway is not represented during the decision-making processes that have direct consequences for it, and neither does Norway have any significant influence over the EU[82].

The ability of people having unrestricted movement for the purposes of trade and labor within the EU is also seen as another remarkable achievement for the EU. While it has allowed for individual liberty and increased economic growth within the EU, there are speculations as to its viability when it is viewed as a negative instance. For example many of the British believe that a flood of immigrants into the UK will decrease the opportunities for the future of the local job market[83].

However, an authoritative study suggests that the movement of EU immigrants into the UK has been a net fiscal contributor[84], paying about a third more in taxes than they received in benefits (in addition to the UK being enriched with an increase in the number of highly educated and skilled immigrants[85]). That, however, is for European welfare states and not

---

[80] C. Archer, 'Norway outside the European Union: Norway and European integration from 1994 to 2004' Routledge, 2005, p179

[81] Ibid

[82] Outside and Inside: Norway's Agreements with the European Union, Official Norwegian Reports NOU 2012: 2 (17 January 2012)
<http://www.regjeringen.no/upload/UD/Vedlegg/eu/nou2012_2_chapter13.pdf>

[83] J. Jones, 'Immigration: Britons Want 'Drastic Action' Sky News 14 October 2013
<http://news.sky.com/story/1153164/immigration-britons-want-drastic-action>

[84] C. Dustmann, & T. Frattini, 'The Fiscal Effects of Immigration to the UK', Discussion Paper Series CDP No 22/13, Centre for Research and Analysis of Migration, Depart.of Economics, University College London <http://www.cream-migration.org/publ_uploads/CDP_22_13.pdf>

[85] Ibid, p.29

'freedom of movement across borders' that conservatives need to address[86]. EU law provides that the free movement of persons is a fundamental right which is guaranteed to EU citizens by virtue Article 45 TFEU[87] and expanded upon[88] in the cases of *Walrave & Koch*[89], *Bosman*[90], *Angonese*[91]

The concept of freedom of movement came about with the Schengen Agreement in 1985 and the subsequent Schengen Convention in 1990 which allowed for Schengen cooperation that is gradually being extended to include most EU Member States as well as some non-EU countries[92], except for the UK[93].

As can be seen (*supra*), the EU's supremacy has not only altered the pattern of law within the UK, but it has also assisted the UK (and other Member States) in areas concerning, capital, economic growth, a common market place, freedom of movement of trade and people, healthcare, having a stronger voice to the rest of the world etc. However this has not been enough for the British, given the recent news of the UK's desire to leave the EU[94].

3.2   The EU's effect on the UK

Of course, with the large business generation that the EU has implemented by way of its common market, it has to be questioned if the UK should leave at all. But given the wide

---

[86] *Ibid*

[87] Article 45 TFEU; '*Free movement of goods: Guide to the application of Treaty provision governing the free movement of goods*', European Commissions Director of Enterprise and Industry (2010) , pg 31 < http://ec.europa.eu/enterprise/policies/single-market-goods/files/goods/docs/art34-36/new_guide_en.pdf>

[88] Vertical and horizontal direct effect of Art. 45 TFEU

[89] (Case 36/74) Walrave and Koch [1974] ECR 1405

[90] (Case C-415/93) Bosman [1995] ECR I-4921 - Free movement of workers

[91] (Case 281/98) Roman Angonese v Cassa di Risparmio di Bolzano [2000] ECR I–4139

[92] European Parliament and Council Directive 2004/38/EC of 29 April 2004 on the right of citizens of the Union and their family members to move and reside freely within the territory of the Member States amending Regulation (EEC) No 1612/68 and repealing Directives 64/221/EEC, 68/360/EEC, 72/194/EEC, 73/148/EEC, 75/34/EEC, 75/35/EEC, 90/364/EEC, 90/365/EEC and 93/96/EEC.

[93] European Commission, 'Schengen Area' (19/11/2013) <http://ec.europa.eu/dgs/home-affairs/what-we-do/policies/borders-and-visas/schengen/index_en.htm>

[94] C. Booker, 'David Cameron can only get what he wants by leaving the EU', *The Telegraph* (16 Nov 2013) <http://www.telegraph.co.uk/news/worldnews/europe/eu/10454192/David-Cameron-can-only-get-what-he-wants-by-leaving-the-EU.html>

debate on the UK's membership of the EU, the UK Government initiated an examination and evaluation of the UK's relationship with the EU and aimed to audit EU activities across policy areas and examine the EU's effects on the UK.

The idea behind this evaluation gave way to 'The Fresh Start Project' which aimed to research and propose a new relationship for the UK within the EU that would better meet the interests of the British[95.]

While, Prime Minister David Cameron, assured that on re-election a referendum would be held on the UK's future as a Member State of the EU in 2015, this has been contradicted recently by the Labour Party who stated that this would only take place *"if there is a proposal to transfer powers away from the UK to the bloc,...something that is unlikely to occur this decade or before 2020..*[96] . However it would be best if the government allowed for a referendum given that number of people in favour of the UK's withdrawal from the EU, with opposition numbers set at 56% in November 2012 compared to the odd 30% who wanted to remain within the EU[97].

In the British Prime Minister's speech he confirmed that (if the Conservatives won the 2015 election) there would be an in/out referendum by 2017 on EU membership, after the Government had renegotiated a new settlement for the UK to exist in a more flexible EU which will incorporate, *"the freedom of a Member State to be flexible in its cooperation with respect for national differences and not trying to eliminate them; to be free of spurious regulation; to be subject to democratic legitimacy and accountability of national parliaments; and it allows for some power to be returned to Member States"*[98]

---

[95] V. Miller, 'Leaving the EU' Research Paper 13/42, House of Commons Library (1 July 2013)

[96] T. King, 'EU referendum unlikely under Labour says Ed Miliband', EuropeanVoice (12 March 2014) <http://www.europeanvoice.com/article/2014/march/uk-labour-party-would-offer-eu-referendum/80005.aspx>

[97] D. Boffey '56% of Britons would vote to quit EU in referendum, poll finds' The Observer (17 November 2012) < http://www.theguardian.com/politics/2012/nov/17/eu-referendum-poll>

[98] EU Speech at Bloomberg 23 January 2013 < https://www.gov.uk/government/speeches/eu-speech-at-bloomberg>

While the UK's membership of the EU has long been a controversial one, some politicians are of the belief that the UK would be better off outside the political and economic arena of the EU and therefore supports the decision for the UK to seek a withdrawal from the EU altogether for the reason set out above[99].

3.3   The procedure to withdraw from EU membership

In the past commentary on the procedure for a Member State leaving the EU has indicated that there were three specific reasons as to why the Treaties were silent on withdrawal. 1) It avoided a Member State having second thoughts on its commitment to the EU. 2) It provided the possibility of withdrawal and would have increased its probability, and three, it would have provided for a withdrawal possibility and added the burden of setting out the lengthy procedure and consequences of withdrawal[100].

Before the Treaty of Lisbon[101] there was no precedent set or provision within the Treaties or EU law that prescribed the ability of a Member State to voluntarily withdraw from the EU. However within the European Constitution there was such provision. But after it failed to be ratified, this provision was included in the Lisbon Treaty[102]. It was apparent that if there was no provision made to accommodate a Member State's decision to withdraw from the EU it would have made it very difficult to exit from the agreement/membership but not impossible[103]

---

[99] J. Springford, & S. Tilford , 'The Great British trade off : The impact of leaving the EU on the UK's trade and investment', Centre for European Reform, (January 2014)
<http://www.cer.org.uk/sites/default/files/publications/attachments/pdf/2014/pb_britishtrade_16jan14-8285.pdf>
[100] H. Scott, 'When the Euro Falls Apart', 1-2 International Finance (1998), p. 215.
[101] Which entered into force on 1 December 2009
[102] D Spinant, "Giscard Forum to Unveil Controversial EU 'Exit Clause'," EuropeanVoice.com, April 3, 2003, http://www. europeanvoice.com/article/imported/giscard-forum-set-to-unveil-controversial-eu-exit-clause-/47086.aspx.
[103] P. Athanassiou, European Central Bank: 'Withdrawal and expulsion from the EU and EMU: some reflections', Legal Working Paper 10, December 2009,
<http://www.ecb.europa.eu/pub/pdf/scplps/ecblwp10.pdf>

A research study suggests that there are only two interpretations on the determination of whether a Member State may withdraw from the EU[104]:

1) That sovereign states have a right to withdraw from their international commitments; and

2) That the Treaties exist and do not have an expiry date, thus there is no provision for a withdrawal where a burden of commitment is placed upon a Member State for an "ever closer union". Typically such a union cannot exist if there is a unilateral withdrawal. The Vienna Convention on the Law of Treaties[105] states that where a party wishes to withdraw unilaterally from a Treaty that does not provide for secession, there are only two cases where withdrawal is allowed:

    a. where all parties recognise an informal right to do so; and

    b. where the situation has changed so completely, that the obligations of a signatory have been radically transformed[106].

Since the Treaty of Lisbon came into force, Member States now have the option to separate themselves from the EU as a result of Article 50 TEU which provides that "*Any Member State may decide to withdraw from the Union in accordance with its own constitutional requirements.*" The prescribed procedure borne of Article 50 TFEU requires a Member State to formally notify the European Council of its intention to secede from the EU. The terms of a

---

[104] T. L. Oliver, "Europe without Britain: Assessing the Impact on the European Union of a British Withdrawal". Stiftung Wissenshaft und Politik/German Institute for International & Security Affairs., (September 2013)
[105] Vienna Convention on the law of Treaties, Section 3Termination and suspension of the Operation of Treaties, Article 54, 'Termination of or withdrawal from a treaty under its provision or by consent of the parties', (23 May 1969)
< https://treaties.un.org/doc/Publication/UNTS/Volume%201155/volume-1155-I-18232-English.pdf>
[106] T. L. Oliver, "*Europe without Britain: Assessing the Impact on the European Union of a British Withdrawal*". Stiftung Wissenshaft und Politik/German Institute for International & Security Affairs., (September 2013)
<http://www.swp-berlin.org/fileadmin/contents/products/research_papers/2013_RP07_olv.pdf>

withdrawal agreement are then negotiated between teams representing the EU and the withdrawing Member State[107].

The Treaties would then cease to be applicable to that Member State either from the date of the agreement or within two years of the notification to the European Council unless the Member State and the Council both agree to extend this period.

The agreement is then concluded by the European Council (on behalf of the EU) and sets out the arrangements for withdrawal, including the framework within which the Member State's future relations and dealings with the EU will be set out. These relate to the UK securing free trade relationships with the EU, membership of the EEA or the possibility of bilateral agreements between Member States. This is then approved by a qualified majority of the European Council, and followed by the consent of the European Parliament. The same procedure is employed should a former Member State seek to rejoin the EU[108].

This diplomatic process allows for a negotiated withdrawal due to the difficulties involved in leaving the EU particularly for economic reasons. However, a Member State's unilateral right to withdraw exists within the operation of Article 50 TEU where the Member State's duties and obligations cease to exist two years after its notification to withdraw to the European Council. This would accordingly not depend on any agreement being concluded.

However, as has been documented by the House of Commons[109], the complexities involved in the withdrawal of the UK from the EU would involve lengthy negotiations over the UK's

---

[107] P. Athanassiou, European Central Bank: '*Withdrawal and expulsion from the EU and EMU: some reflections*', Legal Working Paper 10, December 2009,
<http://www.ecb.europa.eu/pub/pdf/scplps/ecblwp10.pdf>

[108] Open Europe, The Lisbon Treaty and the European Constitution: A Side-by-Side Comparison (2008), 46, http://www.ecln.net/ documents/lisbon/lisbon_-_constitution_side_by_side_open_ europe.pdf.; Athanassiou, P., European Central Bank: 'Withdrawal and expulsion from the EU and EMU: some reflections', Legal Working Paper 10, December 2009,
<http://www.ecb.europa.eu/pub/pdf/scplps/ecblwp10.pdf>

[109] House of Commons, 'The future of the European Union: UK Government policy' Foreign Affairs Committee, First Report of Session 2013 – 2014, Vol.II Oral and Written Evidence (26.6.2012 – 6.2.2013) < http://www.publications.parliament.uk/pa/cm201314/cmselect/cmfaff/87/87ii.pdf>

future relations with the EU with the added expense of the UK realigning legislation to a national level[110].

3.4   The UK's Options

The UK has alternate plans to 'having its say' when it comes to matters of trade and the common single market[111].

The one option available to the UK is that it might seek to rejoin the EFTA and remain within the EEA. This would allow the UK to benefit from the common single market, meaning that it would have an uninterrupted continuation of free movement of people, capital, goods and services[112].

The other option, it may decide to proceed as an individualized country similar to that of Switzerland (which is a member of the EFTA, but not of the EEA) or Norway (which is a member of both the EFTA and the EEA) and negotiate a set of 'personalised' bilateral agreements with the EU on a case-by-case basis. No matter the terms and conditions of the agreement, there is a possibility of an exchange between the levels of access to the common single market, the freedom from EU product regulations, social and employment legislation, budgetary contributions and those rights that are afforded to the British through the EU (such as the freedom of movement)[113].

---

[110] V. Miller, 'Leaving the EU' (1 July 2013) Research Paper 13/42, House of Commons Library
[111] Ibid
[112] House of Commons, 'The future of the European Union: UK Government policy' Foreign Affairs Committee, First Report of Session 2013 – 2014, Vol.II Oral and Written Evidence (26.6.2012 – 6.2.2013) < http://www.publications.parliament.uk/pa/cm201314/cmselect/cmfaff/87/87ii.pdf>
[113] Ibid

The UK has benefited through its EU membership by being party to treaties with third countries, mainly for the purposes of trade[114]. These third country alliance agreements would also have to be renegotiated under the UK withdrawal.

The impact of UK's withdrawal would also have a greater effect on economic areas such as agriculture, trade and employment rather than in, education or culture. There is also the risk of EU financing being affected given that the future financing of the EU had been planned on the basis of the UK continuing its membership. It is foreseeable that a series of complicated negotiations as to the financial aspects between the UK and the EU will need to be reviewed before its withdrawal[115].

3.5   The effect of leaving the EU on businesses in the UK

3.5.1   Argument against the withdrawal of the UK

Fontagene[116] suggests that there has been a positive outlook of the economy with the growth of foreign investment as a result of the UK holding membership with the EU. Many of the large economies such as the USA, China, Indian and Japan have held the UK as their means of a doorway for trade into the EU. The US has expressed their concern on the UK leaving the EU and pointed out an exit from the EU would be a sign that the UK was becoming more isolationist, they believe that the 'UK's participation in the EU is an expression of its influence and its role in the world'[117], i.e. it has a strong influence at the EU table.

---

[114] European Movement UK: 'The Wider Benefits of UK Membership of the EU' (Feb 2012) <http://www.euromove.org.uk/index.php?id=17942>
[115] *Ibid*
[116] L. Fontagne, *'Foreign Direct Investment and International Trade: Complements or substitutes?'* OECD Science, Technology and Industry Working Papers 1999/03, p19 < http://www.oecd-ilibrary.org/docserver/download/5lgsjhvj7n0r.pdf?expires=1396155581&id=id&accname=guest&chec ksum=A13DB67C8AB64A9ED910DAC367FD1260>
[117] I. Harman, 'Obama warns Britain that leaving the EU would be an isolationist step' *The Spectator* (13 May 2013), http://blogs.spectator.co.uk/coffeehouse/2013/05/obama-warns-britain-that-leaving-the-eu-would-be-an-isolationist-step/

There is a real danger for the UK's economy because of the fear of uncertainty that it has caused in the run-up to a proposed referendum which could cause foreign companies to divert or postpone their business investments in the UK. The likes of Unilever[118] and Ford[119], being two of the UK's leading foreign business investors, has warned that they will have to assess their future presence in the UK if the UK had to leave the EU. The CEO in his statement to the Telegraph[120], expressed that "*the UK would be cutting its nose off to spite its face by exiting the EU. He claimed it would be calamitous for British jobs and business*".

Research[121] indicates that the long term effect (to withdraw from the EU), would be that business investment, production and trade may be intentionally directed away from the UK towards other Member States for no other reason than the attractive rights of free trade within the EU where goods are able to move freely without any border controls or tariffs. For example, a mobile phone that is bought in China need only have one fixed tariff charged for it and then be traded over again freely within the EU without any further tariffs being imposed.

Furthermore, UK businesses will have to bear the brunt of additional tariff costs and compliance measures when importing goods from the EU. These measures could be expensive since there would be less investments coming into the UK[122]. This would undoubtedly slow down the UK's technical progress as well as its innovation prowess.

---

[118] J. Rankin, 'EU exit could see Unilever cut investment in the UK' *The Guardian*, (21 January 2014) <http://www.*theguardian*.com/business/2014/jan/21/unilever-warning-uk-withdrawal-european-union>

[119] K. Rushton, 'Ford warns it would reassess UK presence if the country left the EU' *The Telegraph* (14 Jan 2014) < http://www.telegraph.co.uk/finance/economics/10572731/Ford-warns-it-would-reassess-UK-presence-if-country-left-EU.html>

[120] *Ibid*

[121] Bridges Ventures Research, 'The Power of Advice in the UK Sustainable and Impact Investment Market (June 2012) <http://www.bridgesventures.com/sites/bridgesventures.com/files/BV001_Bridges_Ventures_report_final.pdf>

[122] *Ibid*

The UK would also lose the protection the Treaties afforded it. For example the right to the freedom of movement of goods under Article 35 of the TFEU which is guaranteed by virtue of the case of Cassis de Dijon[123].

3.5.2 Argument for the withdrawal of the UK

On the other hand, there are some who argue for leaving the EU which works in the UK's favour by attracting business to the UK on the basis that many will want to steer clear of the EU's unstable economy environment.

Thus the pros to investing are because *"the UK is a very open economy, ... It has deep capital markets and a large number of publicly-listed businesses; and its citizens speak English – all of which make it an attractive place to invest"*[124].

If the UK does in fact withdraw from the EU and establishes a stable economic environment for foreign investment, this could strengthen its currency and provide for a safer trade market than of the EU. However, within the business world, there is always an opportunity for business and a possibility that the UK could forge a mutual trading relationship with the EU whereby it would allow for grounds (perhaps 'investor privilege') within which a foreign investor would see the opportunity that dealing with the UK would also create a door open to investing with the EU for example by waiving tariffs.

For this to happen agreements held between EFTA and the EU would have to be negotiated for a legal way to allow such investment opportunity. Here the UK would exercise its supremacy/control over the decision of when it should allow for its investors to invest within

---

[123] *Rewe Zentrale v Bundesmonopolverwaltung für Branntwein* [1979] ECR 649; as stated above the CJEU established the principle of mutual recognition whereby goods from domestic and foreign traders that are produced and manufactured lawfully by a Member State should circulate freely within the Union without hindrance and unlawful measures.

[124] CER, 'The Great British Trade-Off: The Impact of Leaving the EU on the UK''s Trade and Investment' (January 2014) p.3
<http://www.cer.org.uk/sites/default/files/publications/attachments/pdf/2014/pb_britishtrade_16jan14-8285.pdf>

the EU. However this model would require much thought given the nature of the financial market areas of the UK and the EU.

On the point of the financial and banking sector, it should be noted that the financial services trade is an area of particular importance that may be affected by a Swiss model approach if the UK chose to use it.

For example, non-EEA financial services providers will have to establish a branch within the EU so that it will be able to provide cross-border services. The developments within EU-level financial regulation will make financial services to the EU from outside the EEA more difficult (to avoid another crisis). Thus non-EEA finance providers will be restricted on the variety of services that they can offer the EU after they have registered with the European Securities Markets Authority[125]

3.5.3 An alternate option

There would be a few options to include in its negotiations for withdrawal. For example, free trade movement (*supra*) is something it should retain given then the benefits that is already provided for in present regulation.

Another point to note is that it would be in the UK's favour to investigate its options as Norway and Switzerland has, given their successful economies, as a result of their independence from the EU. But it is doubtful that the UK would be happy with either Swiss or Norwegian models[126]. Norway is one that contributes to EU programmes but has chosen to be bound by EU regulations without having the ability to vote on it. Norway is therefore deemed as a limited EU-influencer and this would be a problem for the UK given its supremacy issues where it would rather lead than follow.

---

[125] the requirements of which will be a strict and difficult one to fulfill.

[126] D. Hannan, 'Switzerland is a more attractive model than Norway, but Britain could be better than either' *The Telegraph* (15 Dec 2012)
<http://blogs.telegraph.co.uk/news/danielhannan/100194407/outside-the-eu-we-should-aim-to-copy-switzerland-not-norway/>

The Swiss model however (which the UK can customize), would seem to be more preferred by the UK given that the Swiss negotiated separate arrangements with the EU, giving it reasonable allowance to pick and choose its terms of agreement.

3.5.4   Impact on the world

The impact of the UK's decision to withdraw is not limited to the EU, but is also extended to the rest of the world. Thus many third country relationships and agreements would need to be adjusted in order to continue mutual relationships. However once the UK has withdrawn from the EU it will have less power to negotiate. Perhaps it is an option for the UK to rejoin the EFTA[127] and adopt its (already active and successful) agreements, while national interest is behind the idea[128].

However, the UK may feel limited by this option as it was not part of the process of shaping the EFTA after it left in 1973.

Whatever it option it so chooses, once the UK's final decision has been made it will determine the outcome of the state of affairs on a global scale not just within the euro-zone.

---

[127] C., Daley, 'Civitas :The European Free Trade Area (EFTA) and the European Economic Area (EEA)' (October 2010) <http://www.civitas.org.uk/eufacts/download/EC.13.EFTAandEEA.pdf>
[128] R, Oulds '71% said they would prefer Britain to leave the EU and join the EFTA' (17 July 2013) The Bruges Group <http://www.brugesgroup.com/eu/71-said-they-would-prefer-britain-to-leave-the-eu-and-join-efta.html?keyword=16>

Chapter 4.
THE SEPARATION OF THE UK FROM THE EU

4.1   The withdrawal process

As discussed above, in terms of Article 50 TEU the UK is allowed to unilaterally leave the EU in accordance with its constitutional requirements which would entail having Parliament by way of an Act repeal the EU law that it integrated into its system, i.e. the European Communities Act 1972 and thereafter put in place a negotiated agreement with the EU on their future working relationship[129].

It is the UK's duty to notify the European Council of its intention to withdraw. In turn the European Council has guidelines for the EU to follow which provides that the EU should negotiate and conclude an agreement, in terms of Article 218(3) TFEU, with the UK setting out the terms and conditions of its withdrawal and taking into consideration the framework and structure of such relationship. Article 218(3) TFEU provides that:

"*The Commission, or the High Representative of the Union for Foreign Affairs and Security Policy where the agreement envisaged relates exclusively or principally to the common foreign and security policy, shall submit recommendations to the Council, which shall adopt a decision authorising the opening of negotiations and, depending on the subject of the agreement envisaged, nominating the Union negotiator or the head of the Union's negotiating team*".

The UK's decision to leave is not dependent on the consideration of the other Member States within the EU neither does it require their endorsement as its withdrawal can occur whether or not there is a withdrawal agreement in place. However, it is in the best interest of the UK

---

[129] V. Miller, 'Leaving the EU' Research Paper 13/42, House of Commons Library (1 July 2013) <www.parliament.uk/briefing-papers/rp13-42.pdf>

and the EU if the terms and conditions of the withdrawal agreement are negotiated as prescribed within Article 50 TEU.

Should the UK wish to withdraw from the EU it must notify the European, which will consider the matter and set out negotiating guidelines. The EU will then conduct negotiations with the UK and draft an agreement setting out the terms and conditions of the UK's withdrawal and the framework of its relationship with the EU.

The process leading up to the withdrawal of the UK entails having a long negotiation period and straightening out the complex structure that consists of an EU budget, legal, political, financial, commercial and personal relationships together with duties, liabilities, obligations and rights. The two-year negotiating period would therefore aim to conclude both the withdrawal agreement and any consequent amendments to the EU Treaties.

The UK would then be released from its obligations under the Treaties upon the enforcement of the withdrawal agreement, or two years after its notification to the European Council. However, this negotiating period may be extended amicably by both parties.

During this negotiating period the UK and European Committee would also consider the provisions of Article 8 on the EU's relationship with its neighbours as it may be applicable to the nature of the withdrawal agreement, given that the UK would seemingly continue to remain a part of the European economic and trading environment. On that note, the UK Prime Minister acknowledged the UK's position in his Bloomberg speech[130]: *"If we leave the EU, we cannot of course leave Europe. It will remain for many years our biggest market, and forever our geographical neighbourhood.... We are tied by a complex web of legal commitments"*.

---

[130] EU Speech at Bloomberg 23 January 2013 < https://www.gov.uk/government/speeches/eu-speech-at-bloomberg>

4.1.1   The EU and UK withdrawal agreement

Given the complexity of the withdrawal process, there would have to be an interim agreement put in place while the withdrawal process between the UK and the EU are being negotiated.

It would be difficult for the transition to occur overnight without impediments. Aspects concerning business, projects, joint ventures research facilities and policy regulations, for example the Common Agricultural Policy, would have to be incorporated into a withdrawal agreement for an alternative system to be put in place to avoid any disruptions of agricultural productivity.

Lazowski[131] explains that under the provisions of Article 50(2) there are a few practical issues that need to be looked at during a Member State's withdrawal. Firstly, that three treaties should be negotiated, (1) one for the departing Member State, (2) one to amend the EU Treaties that removes any references to the departing Member State and (3) one to allow the departing member State to join the EFTA (or similar) and remain within the EEA environment. His advice is logical in that:

1) The withdrawal agreement would have to cover a mixture of political and economic areas relevant to the European zone which are shared between the EU, the UK and those remaining Member States (similar to that of a colour spectrum of black, white and grey areas to be factored in);

2) Unlike accession treaties, withdrawal agreements do not form part of EU primary law. Consequently, unless a legal formula is developed, they cannot amend the treaties on which the EU is based unless an international treaty regulating said withdrawal is introduced, and the remaining Member States would have to negotiate between themselves a treaty amending the founding Treaties in order to repeal all provisions referring to the departing Member State. This would

---

[131] A. Lazowski, 'Withdrawal from the European Union and Alternatives to Membership' (2012) Issue 5, European Law Review, p.523-540

attach a legal nature to the process by which the parties of the withdrawal agreement would have to abide by.

3) On the other hand, if the departing Member State felt that it would have to move sooner rather than later to the EEA there would be further complications to be considered as this would entail a third treaty to be negotiated that regulates the terms of accession to EFTA and a subsequent fourth treaty to deal with the accession to the EEA. This, however, would require approval of the EU, its Member States, the Members States of the EEA-EFTA and the departing/joining country. Thus a departing Member State would have to be treated separately as a third country.

4) However for the duration of the above process there would have to be an 'interim/transitional treaty' negotiated with all the aforementioned parties which would legally connect all the amendments to the Treaties and newly formed treaties to allow this interim treaty the ability to operate while the withdrawal negotiations and withdrawal preparations are being work on. This would allow for the UK's day-to-day business to go undisturbed until the formalities are finalised.

4.1.2 Implementations of the withdrawal agreement in the UK

Lazowski[132] explains that while there is no mention of the procedure for ratification of a withdrawal agreement by the Member States, it is still necessary under international legal rules to be taken into account within EU Treaty amendments, whether it eventuates or not.

While the withdrawal agreement would not be subject to any of the constitutional safeguards in the EU Act 2011, it still needs to be ratified. This means it must go before the UK Government and the contents of the withdrawal agreement must be implemented by an Act

---

[132] *Ibid*

of Parliament. Subsequently, the European Communities Act 1972 would be repealed or amended as needed and other legislation which implements EU Law would be repealed should the UK Government not want it part of national law[133].

4.1.3 The rights of businesses and individuals – follow the Greenland example

While there is no precedent to adhere to when a Member State withdraws from the EU, the EU has deeply entrenched its Member States and their citizens with an irreversible 'legal heritage'[134] of EU rights[135]. There are concerns however on whether the rights of businesses and individuals will be retained within the UK's withdrawal agreement and during the withdrawal negotiation process. The answer can be found by looking at the example of Greenland (particularly their fish industry) who withdrew from European Communities in 1985[136].

After Greenland's withdrawal it still received funding from the EU and enjoyed the rights of tariff-free access to the common market fisheries products. However, in return it had to give the European Communities access to Greenland's waters for the duration of the fisheries agreement. Article 198-204 TFEU, *Association of the Overseas Countries and Territories*[137], applies to Greenland, however this is subject to provisions set out in Protocol No. 34[138] annexed to the TFEU on special arrangements for Greenland fisheries.

---

[133] V. Miller, 'Leaving the EU' Research Paper 13/42, House of Commons Library (1 July 2013), p.11 <www.parliament.uk/briefing-papers/rp13-42.pdf>
[134] ECJ, Case C-26/62, van Gend & Loos, 1963 ECR 1
[135] J. Herbst, "Observations on the Right to Withdraw from the European Union: Who are the 'Masters of the Treaties'?", German Law Journal (6:2005), p1755
[136] F. Harhoff, 'Greenland's Withdrawal from the European Communities', (1983), Common Market Law Review, Vol. 20, Issue 1 pp. 13-34
[137] Regulation (EU) No 952/2013 of the European Parliament and of the Council of 9 October 2013 laying down the Union Customs Code
[138] Consolidated versions of the Treaty on European Union and the Treaty on the Functioning of the European Union OJ C 326, 26/10/2012, p. 1–390<http://www.ecb.europa.eu/ecb/legal/pdf/ce32120061229en00010331.pdf>

Article 2 of the Protocol 15[139] attached to the Greenland Treaty made provision for a transitional period during which Greenlanders, non-national residents and businesses with acquired rights under EU law would retain these rights:

> 'The Commission shall make proposals to the Council, which shall act by a qualified majority, for the transitional measures which it considers necessary, by reason of the entry into force of the new arrangements, with regard to the maintenance of rights acquired by natural or legal persons during the period when Greenland was part of the Community and the regularization of the situation with regard to financial assistance granted by the Community to Greenland during that period.'

There are many provisions of EU law that create individual rights which are directly enforceable in national courts (and the CJEU) whether by horizontal effect between private individuals or vertical effect by an individual against the state). These EU law provisions and principles cover important areas such as the free movement of workers, free movement of goods and freedom of establishment. Given the nature of these rights it should be enforced after the UK's withdrawal and the withdrawal agreement is likely to include these. Even if it is only the very substance of these EU rights that are retained.

Thus to avoid the danger of creating a situation where UK citizens working in EU countries become illegal immigrations and the rights of UK businesses, farmers and fisheries being excluded from EU common policies, trade and funding, it would be necessary for the UK to review the legal privileges, rights, duties and obligations that Greenland observed and follow suit within the UK's withdrawal agreement. Such provisions would also have to be made within an interim or transitional agreement to avoid creating problems of illegality. The provisions of Article 50 TEU allow for the required framework to be taking into account for a withdrawing Member State's future relationship with the EU.

---

[139]Consolidated version of Treaty on the Functioning of the European Union, OJC 321, 29.12.2006, p254 <http://www.ecb.europa.eu/ecb/legal/pdf/ce32120061229en00010331.pdf>

The geographical proximity to its neighbouring countries will dictate that the UK retain many of the EU rules and principles since there are large amounts of EU laws (such as legal rules surrounding the common market, trade, and freedom of movement derived from case law as in *van Gend & Loos*[140]) entrenched into the UK's legal system already.

4.1.4 The EFTA or EEA as an option

While it is a possibility available to the UK, research[141] provides that advocates of a UK withdrawal from the EU have looked into options of multi-lateral or bilateral agreements such as the EFTA and EEA (i.e. Norwegian and Swiss models) but they have found that these arrangements would not be deemed appropriate for the UK if it were to leave the EU because, in both model cases, a non-EU country was obliged to adopt some or all of the body of EU Single Market law with no effective power to influence it (here again is an example of an issue the UK has with the EU's supremacy – a take it or leave it policy). However the aforementioned research concluded that it would be in the UK's best interests if it remained within the EU but demand for a *'radical institutional change in Europe to give decision-making rights in the Single Market to all its participating (Member) states'*[142]

4.1.5 Define the EFTA & EEA

For the purposes of this paper the EFTA is defined as a free trade area, rather than a customs union like that of the EU. Member States[143]. They are able to set their own tariffs and can attain independent Free Trade Agreements (FTAs) with other independent countries.

---

[140] (Case C-26/62) *NV Algemene Transporten Expeditie Onderneming van Gend en Loos v Nederlandse Administratis der Belastingen* [1963] ECR 1.

[141] V. Miller, 'Leaving the EU' Research Paper 13/42, House of Commons Library (1 July 2013)p. 17 <www.parliament.uk/briefing-papers/rp13-42.pdf>

[142] *Ibid*

[143] *Ibid*, p.17

At present, the EFTA has 25 free trade agreements with 35 countries[144]. As depicted below in the EFTA's worldwide network diagram[145]:

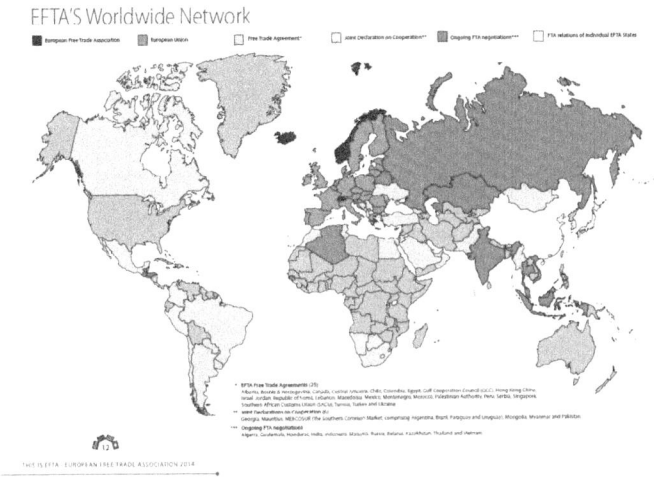

The EFTA official website[146] explains that the EFTA Free Trade Agreements (FTAs) establishes a free trade area between the partners. It provides for free trade in industrial goods, trade with processed agricultural products; trade disciplines; governing preferential trade in goods under the FTA and it elaborates on the rules of customs and origin matters. FTAs therefore open doors for like-minded countries to trade in services, investments and public procurement.

---

[144] EFTA (Publication), 'Free Trade Agreements' < http://www.efta.int/free-trade/free-trade-agreements> (accessed 3.04.2014)
Article 24, paragraph 8 (b) of GATT provides for the definition of the Free Trade Area as"... a group of two or more customs territories in which the duties and other restrictive regulations of commerce are eliminated on substantially all the trade between the constituent territories in products originating in such territories." < http://www.cvce.eu/content/publication/2006/4/20/98aa88e9-ee3a-4494-b11c-0646a0627692/publishable_en.pdf>
[145] EFTA (Publication), 'Free Trade Agreements' < http://www.efta.int/free-trade/free-trade-agreements> (accessed 3.04.2014) p.12
[146] EFTA (Publication), 'Free Trade Agreements' < http://www.efta.int/free-trade/free-trade-agreements> (accessed 3.04.2014)

The EEA is different to the EFTA in that the EEA Agreement is a regional free trade agreement[147] which guarantees equal rights and obligations within an internal market for EEA citizens and economic operators. In order for it to work, non-EU EEA countries must make annual financial contributions to the EU to access its single market. The EEA Agreement also covers areas of cooperation in research, development, education, social policy, the environment, consumer protection, tourism and culture. However its distinctive nature does not cover EU policies on: common agriculture and fisheries, customs union, common trade, common foreign and security, justice and home affairs (regardless of the EFTA countries being a part of the Schengen area), or the monetary union.

Therefore, it is not possible to be a party to the EEA Agreement without being a member of either the EU or EFTA. If the UK so wished it would have to rejoin the EFTA once it left the EU in order to remain in the EEA. However, there are ways and means by which a multi-lateral agreement can be negotiated – similar to the Swiss model where the UK would be able to pick and choose its terms of agreement[148]. For example, Article 127[149] of the EEA Agreement might allow the UK a continuance of free trade and movement between a withdrawing state and the EEA for 12 months after a Member State signals its withdrawal. Perhaps there would be room for the UK to establish a longer or permanent arrangement.

The pro's to the aforementioned scenario is that in remaining with the EEA, UK citizens would be able to work in EU agencies, but would be excluded from working within the main EU institutions.

---

[147] EFTA, 'EEA Agreement - 2014' < http://www.efta.int/eea/eea-agreement>
[148] Although Switzerland is not part of the EEA, their citizens still enjoy the same rights as the those that are citizens of countries of the EEA
[149] EEA Agreement, *OJ No L 1, 3.1.1994, p. 3; and EFTA States' official gazettes* < http://www.efta.int/media/documents/legal-texts/eea/the-eea-agreement/Main%20Text%20of%20the%20Agreement/EEAagreement.pdf>

4.2 The Norwegian or Swiss model

4.2.1 Norwegian Model

There is much controversy around the idea of whether the Norwegian model is the best fit for the UK after it leaves the EU. As discussed above, the UK could follow the Norwegian model, however, the long term effects of this model are not in the best interests of the UK for the following reasons: Firstly, Norway has had to adopt almost 75% of EU laws, labour market rules (such as the working time directive) to crime and policing measures[150].

Secondly, aside from being pressured to accept all EU laws, Norway is disadvantaged as it lacks representation within the EU's institutions and therefore cannot hold any voice of influence in the decision-making process to reflect its own national interests. Thus if the UK even considered the option of 'being Norwegian' it would have to continue to accommodate the EU's retail finance market, but have no voice over the EU regulation governing that market. Furthermore it would have to accept EU employment law which is already an expense the UK bears and still have no way of influencing it.

Finally, on the one hand, Norwegian companies face expenses in the form of tariffs on any imports that contain components from outside the EU when selling *manufactured* goods to the EU (this stems from the EU's hidden laws on rules of origin). On the other hand Norway does not suffer with this and accepts such regime given that 62% of its goods' exports are in the form of fish or natural resources such as oil, which are *not* affected by these rules. However, if these rules were applied to the UK its market for car manufacturing or pharmaceuticals industries would bring sudden additional costs and an economic competitive disadvantage[151].

---

150 *"Norway is not a member of the European Union. That said, Norway is heavily involved in EU integration, and has adopted much EU legislation"* Outside and Inside: Norway's agreements with the European Union, Official Norwegian Reports NOU 2012: 2, (*Unofficial Translation – December 2012*) p.3 <http://www.regjeringen.no/upload/UD/Vedlegg/eu/nou2012_2_chapter03.pdf>
151 *Ibid*

In return for adhering to EU regulations, Norway has control of its farming and fishing industries giving it large economic benefits which assist the country to manage and maintain its heritage. This scenario would not suit the UK given that fishing and farming only account for 0.7% of UK GDP[152]. Given the supremacy the EU policies purport to have the upper-hand over these areas of Norwegian industry, it is not an ideal fit for the UK[153].

EEA membership for the UK means that the UK government will no longer be bound by EU laws and if the UK leaves the EU then the government will be free to amend or repeal the Acts adopted to give effect to the EU laws that are not included in the EEA.

However it would still remain subject to many of the same EU regulations as it presently is but with a lot less influence over the contents of those regulations[154].

4.2.2 Swiss Model

On the face of it, the Swiss model appears to be more attractive to many Eurosceptics because it provides a flexible arrangement through a framework of bilateral agreements which may better preserve the UK's sovereignty; however it may still not be in the best interests of UK[155]. One example is that there would be a limited access to the Single Market for the UK's large services sector and it would be forced to accept EU regulation on same[156].

However the Swiss model allows for the terms and conditions of its bilateral agreements to be discussed on a case-by-case basis, depending on the political will of the parties. And it

---

[152] The United Kingdom Operational Programme for the European fisheries Fund (2007 – 2013) (updated in October 2012)
<http://ec.europa.eu/fisheries/cfp/eff/op/list_of_operational_programmes/uk_en.pdf>
153 Dr C. Burns, '*The Implications for UK Environmental Policy of a Vote to Exit the EU*' (May 2013)
<http://www.foe.co.uk/sites/default/files/downloads/eu_referendum_environment.pdf>
[154] Official Journal of the European Union, L 130 of 29. 4.2004
[155]D. Buchan, 'Outsiders on the inside – Swiss and Norwegian lessons for the UK' Centre for European Reform (September 2012)
<http://www.cer.org.uk/sites/default/files/publications/attachments/pdf/2012/buchan_swiss_norway_1 1oct12-6427.pdf>
[156] House of Commons, Foreign Affairs Committee '*The future of the European Union: UK Government policy*' Oral and written evidence, First report of session: 2013-14, Vol. 2

has close relations with the EU on political, economic and cultural levels. These relationships are governed by a framework of bilateral agreements such as the Free Trade Agreement of 1972[157], the Insurance Agreement of 1989[158] and series of Bilateral Agreements I of 1999 and the Bilateral Agreements II of 2004.

However, the Swiss model does not allow for the UK to have an influence over the decision-making process as it does now while within the EU. A Swiss-model would allow for the UK to be separate from the EU but still expect it to adapt to the regulations of the EU without a voice to influence it, and its position would be further compromised because the UK is considered a large influence when it comes to governing its own interests.

4.2.3 A renegotiation of terms

In his Bloomberg speech[159], Prime Minister David Cameron claimed that his preferred option is to renegotiate the terms and conditions of the UK's EU membership. He argued that if he is successful, on re-election, he will campaign for a yes vote, which means that he will advocate for:

"A new settlement subject to the democratic legitimacy and accountability of national parliaments where Member States combine in flexible cooperation, respecting national differences not always trying to eliminate them and in which we have proved that some powers can in fact be returned to Member States. In other words, a settlement which would be entirely in keeping with the mission for an updated European Union ... More flexible, more adaptable, more open - fit for the challenges of the modern age"[160]

---

[157] Free Trade Agreement 1972 – OJ L300, 31/12/1972, p.0189 - 0280

[158] Agreement between the EEC and the Swiss Confederation on direct insurance other than life assurance – OJ L205, 27/07/1991 p.0003 - 0027

[159] EU Speech at Bloomberg 23 January 2013 < https://www.gov.uk/government/speeches/eu-speech-at-bloomberg>

[160] EU Speech at Bloomberg 23 January 2013 < https://www.gov.uk/government/speeches/eu-speech-at-bloomberg>

This would surely allow for the UK to curtail the supremacy issues it has with the EU and allow for a more democratic rule when it comes to implementing issues of policy and regulation especially where its economy is concerned. Furthermore, it would be in the best interests of the UK, for the reasons stated above, to stay within the EU as it would have 'personal involvement' and influence over the decision-making process as well as route for its own personal interests to be taken into consideration while also having a voice to vote yes or no to the EU's policies. As discussed above, the EU affords a large net of protection rights for its Member States and citizens; this together with the financial factor of withdrawing from the EU could be viewed as a positive to stay within the EU.

4.2.4   Conclusion

If it ever occurred, a referendum to leave (or not) will answer the question of whether the people of the UK want to be in the EU. However there are more far reaching consequences that a UK exit could cause for its environment, economy, people and international standing. Furthermore, there is no precedent for a Member State to leave the EU, so there is no guarantee that the UK will succeed on its own.

As discussed above, there are many assumptions as to whether a Norwegian model or Swiss model would suit. Both do not suit the UK given that either way, the UK would have to stay within EU regulation. However, there is room for the UK to customize its own model of membership.

Perhaps as suggested in the Bloomberg Speech[161] the UK is better within the EU and with negotiation will reform the EU to afford the Member States a voice of influence on decisions, their sovereignty returned to national level and allowance of more flexible policies to assist in

---

[161] EU Speech at Bloomberg 23 January 2013 < https://www.gov.uk/government/speeches/eu-speech-at-bloomberg>

future challenges the EU may face. Matched against these aspects the matter of EU supremacy is not that important an issue to cause the UK to leave the EU[162].

Therefore it is not a simple question of 'Are you in or out?'. Looking forward it would be a great advantage to the UK if its Government provided information to its citizens on its findings as to the options that are available in the event of an exit and the implications arising from each of those options before the proposed referendum so that the British public can make an informed choice for their future.

There is more security in the UK staying within EU as it would continue to be a part of a larger market, with influential power to shape its rules and norms, to have clear outcomes that it wishes to enforce with its own interests in mind, the opportunity to drive its economic growth and to implement a more 'democratic flow of power to a Member State..'. This will ensure its integrity and stability in the eyes of the world as it influences the EU to move progressively towards a secure future.

---

[162] W. Phelan, 'Why do the EU Member States Accept the Supremacy of European Law? Explaining Supremacy as an Alternative to Bilateral Reciprocity', Journal of European Public Policy, .(July 2011), Vol. 18 Issue 5, p766-777.

Bibliography

Books

1. Archer, C. *Norway outside the European Union: Norway and European integration from 1994 to 2004* Routledge, 2005, p179

2. Aust, A., *Chapter 23: The European Union* Handbook of International Law, 2nd Ed. Cambridge University Press, 2010, p.430

3. Archick, K., *The European Union: Questions and Answers* Congressional Research Service, 2014, p.1

4. Boomberg, E. and Stubb, A. *The European Union: How Does It Work*, New York: Oxford University Press, 2003, p. 62

5. Craig P. and De Burca, P. *EU Law Test, Cases and Materials*, 4th Ed. Oxford University Press, 2007, p.344

6. Hanson S., *Chapter 5: Reaching English Law – The European Dimension, Legal Method and Reasoning*, 2nd Ed. CP 2003, p.132

7. Mingst, K. A. , Arreguín-Toft I. M., *Chapter 7: Intergovernmental Organizations, Nongovernmental Organizations, and International Law | Essentials of International Relations*, 5 Ed. 2010 < http://www.wwnorton.com/college/polisci/essentials-of-international-relations5/ch/07/summary.aspx>

8. Newman M., *Concepts and Confusions - Democracy, Sovereignty and the European Union*, London: Hurst & Company, 1996, p.3

Case Law

1. (Case 415/93) *Bosman* [1995] ECR I-4921 - Free movement of workers

2. *Factortame Ltd. v Secretary of State for Transport* [1991] 1 AC 603, 658

3. (Case 6/64) *Flaminio Costa v ENEL* [1964] ECR 585, CMLR 425,593

4. (Case 228/69), *Internationale Handelsgesellschaft mbH v. Einfuhr und Vorratsstelle für Getreide und Futtermittel* [1970] ECR 1125; [1972] CMLR 255

5. *Macarthys Ltd v Wendy Smith* [1980] EUECJ R-129/79 (27 March 1980)

6. (Case C-26/62) *NV Algemene Transporten Expeditie Onderneming van Gend en Loos v Nederlandse Administratis der Belastingen* [1963] ECR 1

7. (Case 281/98) *Roman Angonese v Cassa di Risparmio di Bolzano* [2000] ECR I–4139

8. (Case 106/77), *Simmenthal II* [1978] ECR 629

9. *Rewe Zentrale v Bundesmonopolverwaltung für Branntwein* ('Cassis de Dijon') [1979] ECR 649

10. (Case 36/74) *Walrave and Koch* [1974] ECR 1405

Journal and Peer reviewed articles

1. P. Athanassiou, , "European Central Bank: Withdrawal and expulsion from the EU and EMU: some reflections", December 2009, Legal Working Paper 10, <http://www.ecb.europa.eu/pub/pdf/scplps/ecblwp10.pdf>

2. D. Buchan, "Outsiders on the inside – Swiss and Norwegian lessons for the UK", September 2012, Centre for European Reform <http://www.cer.org.uk/sites/default/files/publications/attachments/pdf/2012/buchan_swiss_norway_11oct12-6427.pdf>

3. Dr C. Burns, "The Implications for UK Environmental Policy of a Vote to Exit the EU" May 2013 <http://www.foe.co.uk/sites/default/files/downloads/eu_referendum_environment.pdf>

4. "The Power of Advice in the UK Sustainable and Impact Investment Market", June 2012, Bridges Ventures Research, <http://www.bridgesventures.com/sites/bridgesventures.com/files/BV001_Bridges_Ventures_report_final.pdf>

5. D. Spinant, "Giscard Forum to Unveil Controversial EU 'Exit Clause'", April 2003, *EuropeanVoice.com* <http://www. europeanvoice.com/article/imported/giscard-forum-set-to-unveil-controversial-eu-exit-clause-/47086.aspx.>

6. F. Delperee *et al*, "Opinion on the 4th Amendment of the Constitution of Hungary" 2011, p.9, <http://www.kormany.hu/download/d/e0/e0000/Traduc%20-%20opinion%20on%204th%20amendment.pdf>

7. M. Dougan "Who Exactly Benefits from the Treaties? The Murky Interaction Between Union and National Competence Over the Capacity to Enforce EU Law" Cambridge Yearbook of European Legal Studies, Vol 12 (2009-2010) pp 73-120

8. C. Dustmann & T. Frattini, "The Fiscal Effects of Immigration to the UK", Discussion Paper Series CDP No 22/13, Centre for Research and Analysis of Migration, Depart. of Economics, University College London <http://www.cream-migration.org/publ_uploads/CDP_22_13.pdf>

9. D. Edward, "EU Law and the Separation of Member States", (2013) 36 Fordham Int'l L.J. 1151

10. L. Fontagne, , "Foreign Direct Investment and International Trade: Complements or substitutes?" OECD Science, Technology and Industry Working Papers 1999/03, p19 < http://www.oecd-ilibrary.org/docserver/download/5lgsjhvj7n0r.pdf?expires=1396155581&id=id&accname=guest&checksum=A13DB67C8AB64A9ED910DAC367FD1260>

11. F. Harhoff, , "Greenland's Withdrawal from the European Communities", (1983), Common Market Law Review, Vol. 20, Issue 1 pp. 13-34

12. Herbst, J., "Observations on the Right to Withdraw from the European Union: Who are the 'Masters of the Treaties'?", German Law Journal (6:2005), p1755

13. Lord Irvine, "Sovereignty in Comparative Perspective: Constitutionalism in Britain and America", New York University Law Review, April 2001, Vol.76, Issue 1, p.1

14. Lazowski, A. 'Withdrawal from the European Union and Alternatives to Membership' (2012) Issue 5, European Law Review, p.523-540

15. J.M. Magone, 'The end of the borders? The politics of territorial cooperation in the multi-level governance system. A comparative study of cross-border cooperation initiatives' Berlin School of Economics & Law (2010) < http://www.aecpa.es/uploads/files/congresos/congreso_09/grupos-trabajo/area02/GT01/08.pdf>

16. A. Matthews, "How Might the EU's Common Agricultural Policy Affect Trade and Development After 2013?" (December 2010). ICTSD. < http://ictsd.org/i/publications/97803/>

17. P. Minford, V. Mahambare, and E. Nowell, 'Should Britain Leave the EU? An Economic Analysis of a Troubled Relationship' http://www.euro-know.org/eu_book/index.php

18. T. L. Oliver, 'Europe without Britain: Assessing the Impact on the European Union of a British Withdrawal". Stiftung Wissenshaft und Politik/German Institute for International & Security Affairs., (September 2013) <http://www.swp-berlin.org/fileadmin/contents/products/research_papers/2013_RP07_olv.pdf>

19. R, Oulds '71% said they would prefer Britain to leave the EU and join the EFTA' (17 July 2013) The Bruges Group http://www.brugesgroup.com/eu/71-said-they-would-prefer-britain-to-leave-the-eu-and-join-efta.html?keyword=16

20. W. Phelan, 'Why do the EU Member States Accept the Supremacy of European Law? Explaining Supremacy as an Alternative to Bilateral Reciprocity', Journal of European Public Policy, .(July 2011), Vol. 18 Issue 5, p766-777

21. H. Scott, 'When the Euro Falls Apart', 1-2 International Finance (1998), p. 215

22. J. Springford, & S. Tilford, , 'The Great British trade off : The impact of leaving the EU on the UK's trade and investment', Centre for European Reform, (January 2014) <http://www.cer.org.uk/sites/default/files/publications/attachments/pdf/2014/pb_british trade_16jan14-8285.pdf>

23. M. Stiernstrom, 'The Relationship between Community Law and National Law' The Jean Monnet Chair University of Miami, Miami Florida (October 2005)

24. B. Vaughan, 'An Analysis of EU Governance and Policy Making', National Economic & Social Development Office NESDO, p.28

25. Prof J.H.H. Weiler, 'The Rule of Law as a Constitutional Principle of the European Union' JeanMonnet Working , Paper 04/09, <www.jeanmonnetprogram.org/archive/papers/09/090401.doc>

Press articles

1. C. Booker, 'David Cameron can only get what he wants by leaving the EU', The Telegraph,16 Nov 2013 <http://www.telegraph.co.uk/news/worldnews/europe/eu/10454192/David-Cameron-can-only-get-what-he-wants-by-leaving-the-EU.html>

2. D. Boffey '56% of Britons would vote to quit EU in referendum, poll finds', The Observer, 17 November 2012 <http://www.theguardian.com/politics/2012/nov/17/eu-referendum-poll>

3. Britain and Europe: Making the break, The Economist, Good-bye Europe Paper Edition 8 December 2012 <http://www.economist.com/news/briefing/21567914-how-britain-could-fall-out-european-union-and-what-it-would-mean-making-break>

4. L.R. Christensen *et al* 'The Impact of the Data Protection Regulation in the E.U.' *The European Financial Review*, 18 June 2013 <http://www.europeanfinancialreview.com/?p=6885>

5. D. Hannan, 'Switzerland is a more attractive model than Norway, but Britain could be better than either', *The Telegraph*, 15 December 2012 <http://blogs.telegraph.co.uk/news/danielhannan/100194407/outside-the-eu-we-should-aim-to-copy-switzerland-not-norway/>

6. I. Harman, 'Obama warns Britain that leaving the EU would be an isolationist step' *The Spectator*, 13 May 2013, <http://blogs.spectator.co.uk/coffeehouse/2013/05/obama-warns-britain-that-leaving-the-eu-would-be-an-isolationist-step/>

7. A. Kaletsky, 'Will Britain leave the European Union', *Reuters*, 16 January 2014 <http://blogs.reuters.com/anatole-kaletsky/2014/01/16/will-britain-really-leave-the-european-union/>

8. J. Rankin, 'EU exit could see Unilever cut investment in the UK', *The Guardian*, 21 January 2014, <http://www.*theguardian*.com/business/2014/jan/21/unilever-warning-uk-withdrawal-european-union>

9. K. Rushton, , 'Ford warns it would reassess UK presence if the country left the EU', *The Telegraph*, 14 January 2014 <http://www.telegraph.co.uk/finance/economics/10572731/Ford-warns-it-would-reassess-UK-presence-if-country-left-EU.html>

10. D. Vasishev, 'Contrary to Perception, the EU is a Boon to Free Markets', *Forbes* March 2013, <http://www.forbes.com/sites/realspin/2014/03/17/contrary-to-perception-the-european-union-is-a-boon-to-free-markets/>

Think tanks, foreign and international organizations

1. CER, 'The Great British Trade-Off: The Impact of Leaving the EU on the UK"s Trade and Investment' (January 2014) p.3 <http://www.cer.org.uk/sites/default/files/publications/attachments/pdf/2014/pb_british trade_16jan14-8285.pdf>

2. Daley, C., 'Civitas :The European Free Trade Area (EFTA) and the European Economic Area (EEA)' (October 2010) http://www.civitas.org.uk/eufacts/download/EC.13.EFTAandEEA.pdf

3. EFTA, 'EEA Agreement - 2014' < http://www.efta.int/eea/eea-agreement> (accessed 3.04.2014)

4. EFTA (Publication), 'Free Trade Agreements' < http://www.efta.int/free-trade/free-trade-agreements> (accessed 3.04.2014)

5. EEA Agreement, OJ No L 1, 3.1.1994, p. 3; and EFTA States' official gazettes < http://www.efta.int/media/documents/legal-texts/eea/the-eea-agreement/Main%20Text%20of%20the%20Agreement/EEAagreement.pdf>

6. European Movement UK: 'The Wider Benefits of UK Membership of the EU' (Feb 2012) http://www.euromove.org.uk/index.php?id=17942

7. 'European Movement UK: The Wider Benefits of UK Membership of the EU' Euromove, (February 2012)

8. Economic and Financial Affairs, ' The euro: Economic and Monetary Union January European Commission, 17 January 2014 <http://ec.europa.eu/economy_finance/euro/emu/index_en.htm>

9. "Outside and Inside: Norway's agreements with the European Union", Official Norwegian Reports NOU 2012: 2, (Unofficial Translation – December 2012) p.3 <http://www.regjeringen.no/upload/UD/Vedlegg/eu/nou2012_2_chapter03.pdf>

House of Commons Library publications

1. House of Commons, 'The future of the European Union: UK Government policy' Foreign Affairs Committee, First Report of Session 2013 – 2014, Vol.II Oral and Written Evidence (26.6.2012 – 6.2.2013) < http://www.publications.parliament.uk/pa/cm201314/cmselect/cmfaff/87/87ii.pdf>

2. Loveland, I. "*Parliamentary Sovereignty and the European Community: The Unfinished Revolution?*" Parliamentary Affairs, Oct. 1996, Vol. 49, Issue 4, p.517

3. Miller, V. 'Leaving the EU' Research Paper 13/42, House of Commons Library (1 July 2013)p. 17 www.parliament.uk/briefing-papers/rp13-42.pdf

Government Publications

1. EU Speech at Bloomberg 23 January 2013 <https://www.gov.uk/government/speeches/eu-speech-at-bloomberg>

2. The United Kingdom Operational Programme for the European fisheries Fund (2007 – 2013) (updated in October 2012) <http://ec.europa.eu/fisheries/cfp/eff/op/list_of_operational_programmes/uk_en.pdf>

Treaties and Legislation

1. Consolidated version of Treaty on the Functioning of the European Union, OJC 321, 29.12.2006, p.254 http://www.ecb.europa.eu/ecb/legal/pdf/ce32120061229en00010331.pdf

2. Consolidated versions of the Treaty on European Union and the Treaty on the Functioning of the European Union OJ C 326, 26/10/2012, p. 1–390 http://www.ecb.europa.eu/ecb/legal/pdf/ce32120061229en00010331.pdf

3. EU Communities Act 1972, c.68, Part 1, Section 2 <http://www.legislation.gov.uk/ukpga/1972/68/section/2 (accessed 23 January 2014)

4. EUR-Lex, '*Accession to the European Communities of the Kingdom of Denmark, Ireland, the Kingdom of Norway and the United Kingdom of Great Britain and Northern Ireland*' OJ L 73 27.3.1972 http://eur-lex.europa.eu/JOHtml.do?uri=OJ:L:1972:073:SOM:EN:HTML

5. European Parliament and Council Directive 2004/38/EC of 29 April 2004 on the right of citizens of the Union and their family members to move and reside freely within the territory of the Member States amending Regulation (EEC) No 1612/68 and repealing Directives 64/221/EEC, 68/360/EEC, 72/194/EEC, 73/148/EEC, 75/34/EEC, 75/35/EEC, 90/364/EEC, 90/365/EEC and 93/96/EEC

6. European Commission, 'Schengen Area' (19/11/2013) http://ec.europa.eu/dgs/home-affairs/what-we-do/policies/borders-and-visas/schengen/index_en.htm

7. EU Union, 'EU Treaties' <http://europa.eu/about-eu/basic-information/decision-making/treaties/index_en.htm> (accessed on: 17/2/2014)

8. *Free movement of goods: Guide to the application of Treaty provision governing the free movement of goods*', European Commissions Director of Enterprise and Industry (2010) , pg 31 < http://ec.europa.eu/enterprise/policies/single-market-goods/files/goods/docs/art34-36/new_guide_en.pdf>

9. *Official Journal Council Regulation (EC) OJ L 73 of 7.3.1972, p. 3 <http://eur-lex.europa.eu/LexUriServ/LexUriServ.do?uri=OJ:L:1972:073:FULL:EN:PDF>*

10. *Official Journal of the European Communities Legislation, Special Edition, 27 March 1972 http://eur-lex.europa.eu/LexUriServ/LexUriServ.do?uri=OJ:L:1972:073:FULL:EN:PDF*

11. Open Europe, The Lisbon Treaty and the European Constitution: A Side-by-Side Comparison (2008), 46, http://www.ecln.net/ documents/lisbon/lisbon_-_constitution_side_by_side_open_ europe.pdf.;

12. Rome Treaty 1957, Title 1, 'Common Provisions, Article 1 < http://eur-lex.europa.eu/en/treaties/dat/12002M/htm/C_2002325EN.000501.html>

13. The Founding Treaties ('FT') being Treaty establishing the European Coal and Steel Community (1951); Treaty establishing European Economic Community (1957); Treaty establishing the European Atomic Energy Community (1957); Treaty on European Union (1992).

14. The 'Treaties':
    a. Treaty of Lisbon, (signed: 13 December 2007, entered into force: 1 December 2009);
    b. Treaty of Nice, (signed: 26 February 2001, entered into force: 1 February 2003);
    c. Treaty of Amsterdam (signed: 2 October 1997, entered into force: 1 May 1999);
    d. Treaty on European Union – Maastricht Treaty (signed: 7 February 1992, entered into force: 1 November 1993);
    e. Single European Act (signed: 17 and 28 February 1986 (in Luxembourg and The Hague respectively), entered into force: 1 July 1987);
    f. Merger Treaty – Brussels Treaty (signed: 8 April 1965, entered into force: 1 July 1967);
    g. Treaties of Rome – EEC and EURATOM treaties (signed 25 March 1957 and entered into force: 1 January 1958);
    h. Treaty establishing the European Coal and Steel Community (signed: 18 April 1951, entered into force: 23 July 1952 – expired 23 July 2002).

15. Regulation (EC) No 2006/2004 of the European Parliament and of the Council of 27 October 2004 on cooperation between national authorities responsible for the enforcement of consumer protection laws (the Regulation on consumer protection cooperation) [See amending act(s)]. <http://europa.eu/legislation_summaries/consumers/protection_of_consumers/l32047_en.htm>

16. Regulation (EU) No 952/2013 of the European Parliament and of the Council of 9 October 2013 laying down the Union Customs Code

17. Vienna Convention on the law of Treaties, Section 3 Termination and suspension of the Operation of Treaties, Article 54, 'Termination of or withdrawal from a treaty under its provision or by consent of the parties', (23 May 1969)
< https://treaties.un.org/doc/Publication/UNTS/Volume%201155/volume-1155-I-18232-English.pdf n